Copyright © 2014 by Jill Johnson

All rights reserved. This publication is not to be reproduced, stored in a mechanical, photocopying, recording, or otherwise, without prior written permission of the publisher.

ISBN # 978-0-9864040-0-9

Printed in the United States of America.

For my family:

Your continual hope for brighter days has been an inspiration to me.

BIPOLAR, DADDY, & ME
Jill Johnson
Illustrated by Michelle Johnson

This book belongs to:

Sammy's mommy is busy.

Sammy's sister, Kate, is talking to her friend.

Sammy is playing with his big, red, fire truck, but he wished his dad could play with him.

Sammy's daddy is sitting in a dark room.

Sammy didn't know why his daddy was sad. He was worried and thought about what he could do.

Suddenly, he had an idea! In his parents' room was an old computer. Sammy knew he wasn't allowed in the room, but he had to find an answer.

So he looked over his shoulder to make sure no one was looking, then tiptoed into his parents' room.

Sammy raced to that old computer and quickly hit a button, but nothing happened. He hit it again, but still, nothing happened. Nervously, he glanced at the door.

Then he pushed the buttons all at once, but still, nothing happened. Perplexed, he shouted, "Open! Open! Open!"

Sammy looked around the computer and underneath the desk. Surprised, he spotted a ...

black box with a small button. He pushed it hard. Suddenly, a loud noise exploded from the computer, which made him JUMP!

Sammy watched as the computer began to rattle and shake. It caused such a stir that he leaped from his seat and ran straight to his room.

Rufus could tell when Sammy isn't himself.

"Hey boy! Do you know why Daddy gets sad?" Rufus let out a bark, but not even Rufus knew.

Finally, Sammy went to Kate and asked, "Why do you think Daddy gets like that?"

"Gets like what?" Kate asked. "Yesterday, Daddy was happy. Today, he is sad. He always gets that way."

"Do you know what bipolar is?" Kate asked.

"No, what's that?" "Well, bipolar is like a mean, old, scary, monster in Dad's brain.

It makes him feel super energetic, and it makes him feel sad."

"Do you mean sadder than when Grandma died?" "He sometimes feels even sadder," Kate answered.

"How do you know that?" Sammy suspiciously whispered. "Because I'm older, I know everything," replied Kate.

When Sammy went to sleep that night, he had a bad dream. Frightened, he called for his mother.

"It's alright, Sammy. Did you have a bad dream?" Sammy nodded.

Sammy's daddy heard the noise and ran into his room.

"Did someone say he had a bad dream? That's not fun." "Daddy! You're safe!" Sammy shouted happily.

"I was afraid that mean, old, scary, bipolar monster would eat us up, and we wouldn't play again."

Puzzled, Sammy's daddy asked, "Who told you that?" "Kate did," answered Sammy.

"Bipolar is not a monster. It's an illness in my brain," Sammy's daddy explained.

"Sometimes it makes me feel depressed or sad. And sometimes, it makes me feel manic or energetic. Like doing many things without feeling tired."

"Can people do a lot without feeling tired?" asked Sammy. "Ordinary people can't, but maybe superheroes can," his daddy laughed.

Sammy laughed too. He understood.

Sammy knew that he would play his favorite game, Fire Truck, with his daddy as soon as he was feeling better.

After a while, Sammy's daddy started to feel GOOD.

Then he felt BETTER.

Eventually, he was at his BEST!

Early one morning, Sammy found his daddy in the kitchen humming.

He grabbed his big, red, fire truck and placed it on the kitchen table for his daddy to see.

"Sammy, race you to the family room."

Giggling, Sammy took off running. Sammy's daddy followed happily behind him.

The End.

www.ingramcontent.com/pod-product-compliance
Lightning Source LLC
LaVergne TN
LVHW072100070426
835508LV00002B/187